a pocketful of

RHYME

Imagination for a new generation

2006 Poetry Competition for 7-11 year-olds

Young Writers

Expressions From
Southern England

Edited by Heather Killingray

 Young**Writers**

First published in Great Britain in 2007 by:
Young Writers
Remus House
Coltsfoot Drive
Peterborough
PE2 9JX
Telephone: 01733 890066
Website: www.youngwriters.co.uk

SB ISBN 978-1 84602 866 3

Foreword

Young Writers was established in 1991 and has been passionately devoted to the promotion of reading and writing in children and young adults ever since. The quest continues today. Young Writers remains as committed to the nurturing of poetic and literary talent as ever.

This year's Young Writers competition has proven as vibrant and dynamic as ever and we are delighted to present a showcase of the best poetry from across the UK and in some cases overseas. Each poem has been selected from a wealth of *A Pocketful Of Rhyme* entries before ultimately being published in this, our fourteenth primary school poetry series.

Once again, we have been supremely impressed by the overall quality of the entries we have received. The imagination, energy and creativity which has gone into each young writer's entry made choosing the poems a challenging and often difficult but ultimately hugely rewarding task - the general high standard of the work submitted ensured this opportunity to bring their poetry to a larger appreciative audience.

We sincerely hope you are pleased with this final collection and that you will enjoy *A Pocketful Of Rhyme Expressions From Southern England* for many years to come.

Contents

Jack Oldroyd (9)   32
Joseph Hellyer (9)   33
James Gibson (9)   34

Stafford Junior School, Eastbourne
Kieran Miller (9)   35
Georgia Bellett (7)   36
Nathan Fuller (10)   37
Lily Crossley (9)   38
Christopher Daniels (10)   39
Zoe Heather (9)   40
Louise Grafham (10)   41
Laurence Cox (9)   42
Rachael Berrisford (9)   43
Caitlin Taylor Hood (10)   44
Holly Ayres (9)   45
Demi-Jade Goodison (9)   46
Chloë Funnell (9)   47
Daniel Wright (9)   48
Rowan Fitzgerald (10)   49
Rosie Pugh (9)   50
Marco Belim (9)   51
Jessica Weston (9)   52
Jordan Ticehurst (9)   53
Lucas Belim (9)   54
Connor Baxter (9)   55
Jude Kean (9)   56
Samantha Irons (9)   57
Oliver Zecchin (10)   58
Danni Lewis (10)   59
Gemma Courtney-Davies (9)   60
Jamie Hill (10)   61
Taelor Roberson (10)   62
Ben Cooper (10)   63
Eleanor Grant (10)   64
Samantha May Avard (10)   65
Charlie Mackay (8)   66
Benjamin Horan (10)   67
Charley Baxter (10)   68
Roxanne Passmore (10)   69
Benito Caira (10)   70

Thomas's Battersea, London

Viking First & Middle School, Northolt

The Poems

Weather

It is sunny today
but will the rain come and play?
We don't know yet, it's not the end of the day.

Something might happen
lightning might strike
but I hope it is not tonight.

But through night and day
we can always play
if it's raining or not.

Reece Hunt (9)
Bobbing Village School, Sittingbourne

I Need A Friend

I need a friend,
Someone sweet,
Who can cheer me up
When I am down,
Someone that will care for me
And give me a shoulder to cry on.

Someone to trust,
Someone to care for,
Someone to cuddle,
Somebody to play with when I am alone.

So please help me find a friend.

Sophie Garry & Lacey Lewis (10)
Fairholme Primary School, Feltham

Miss Willis

I like Miss Willis, she is great
And she is one of my best mates.
When we yelp
She's here to help
She's always here no matter what
That's why we love here a lot.

Great Miss Willis.

Grace Rhodes (10) & Sarah Holland (11)
Fairholme Primary School, Feltham

Wolf

W is for wolf that scares you in the night
O the terrible cry that makes me cry
L is for lollies, how they take you down
F is for flee when you see a wolf.

Jack Hendy & Benjamin Ford (10)
Fairholme Primary School, Feltham

Fairholme School

Fairholme School
Is so cool,
I like to play basketball.

First I have numeracy,
Then it is literacy.

Next it was break,
I had a flake and a cake.

After a while it was history,
After that we learnt about a mystery.

Next it was lunch,
I decided I'd have a munch,
On my crisps and go crunch, crunch, *crunch*.

Then it was home time,
I started to mime,
'Fairholme School is so cool.'

Amy Storey (8)
Fairholme Primary School, Feltham

Vampire

V ermin vampires upsetting children
A liens fly through the sky in a spaceship
M onsters munch you until there is nothing left
P eople scream and run away
I 'm scared to bits
R azor-sharp teeth on vampires
E at people!

Nathan Jeffers (11)
Fairholme Primary School, Feltham

Hallowe'en

October 31st is called Hallowe'en,
What do you do when you can't be seen?
You ring the next door bell and slip out of sight,
When it is spooky, in the middle of the night.

The door creaks open,
What do I see?
A vampire's face staring at me!
What do I do? Shall I scream?
Maybe not or I'm bound to be seen.

I gaze up at the sky, it should be blue,
I look down at my watch, it's quarter-past two.
I should be at home tucked up in my bed,
But I'm eating my Hallowe'en sweets instead!

Tansha Bedi (10) & Krupa Popat (11)
Fairholme Primary School, Feltham

World Cup Poem

It's the day of the World Cup and we're playing the Ivory Coast
Owen loses the ball and Drogba hits the post

Rooney is one on one and on a roll
The keeper spills it and Rooney scores a goal

The final whistle goes and we're through to the next round
The crowd roars, listen to that sound!

We've got to the final and playing Argentina
What a big stadium, it's a massive arena.

We are into stoppage time, with us needing the winner
Lampard scores and that's the killer.

Sam Evans (10)
Fairholme Primary School, Feltham

Hallowe'en Queen

One day the
Hallowe'en queen
Came out to scream
But then she heard a voice
'Trick or treat,' it shouted
The old queen pouted
And said, 'Money for a sweet
Trick or treat!'

Lacie Plowman (10)
Fairholme Primary School, Feltham

Bat And Vampire

B rain pops out when you are scared
A bird that can only see in the dark
T each you how to be a vampire

V ery scary people on Hallowe'en
A scary bat
M ake sure not to go near the sunlight
P eople get scared
I s totally made of dark
R azor-sharp teeth on vampire
E ats people.

Salen Thapa (10)
Fairholme Primary School, Feltham

Lunch Crunch

Lunch I always love to crunch
I love crisps that I always munch
And also the Munch Bunch drink
People come to sit at your table
Say, 'Buzz off little thing'
Eat your lunch and crunch on it.

Benjamin Ford (10)
Fairholme Primary School, Feltham

Poem On Hallowe'en

When it became Hallowe'en
Every place turned green
I could not believe what I had seen
It was the Hallowe'en queen
Then my mum told me to clean
After that she made me a bean
I said to my mum, 'You're so mean
So I walked over to the disappearing machine
Then I went out for trick or treat
I went as a ghost and I had a sheet
When I came in I had some meat
Then I told my mum my work was neat.

Skye Lawrence (11)
Fairholme Primary School, Feltham

Witch

W icked spells are my thing
I fly high on my magic broom
T he wind rushes through my hair
C reepy but cool trees stand outside my mansion
H allowe'en is my favourite day because I'm a . . .

Witch!

Louise Ivey (10)
Fairholme Primary School, Feltham

Scream

S cary skeleton stabs you
C ats are killed by skeletons
R azor-sharp teeth on vampires
E ats people with anarchy
A nts become big and kill you
M onsters throw rocks at you.

Frank Kolaj (10)
Fairholme Primary School, Feltham

Ghost

Once there was a funny ghost
Which loved to eat lots of toast
He went to the coast
And hung on a post
Once there was a funny ghost.

Gabriella Fenlon (10)
Fairholme Primary School, Feltham

Poem Of Hallowe'en

On the 31st of October it was Hallowe'en,
I really wanted to meet the Hallowe'en queen,
I knew that she had hair that was green,
Just so I was going to the freaky machine,
My mum called, 'Come here daughter and clean.'

Hallowe'en is all about trick or treat!
I was a ghost with a long white sheet,
Before I went back out I had something to eat,
Whilst I was eating something grabbed my feet,
It was so hot, 76 degrees was the heat.

Charlotte Pursey (10)
Fairholme Primary School, Feltham

Astronaut

A liens
S pace
T errestrial
R ocket
O rbit
N eptune
A stronaut
U niverse
T ransmission.

Jake Murphy (9)
Fairholme Primary School, Feltham

Fred

I was such a fool
To skip merrily on my first day at school
I met this boy
His name was Fred
He had a very ugly head
I looked at him and rolled my eyes
When he saw me he replied
'Hello, alright,
You what? Am I polite.'
He would talk to me all day
I would never get the time to play
This went on for weeks and weeks
I never had the time to sleep!
Then one day I just had to pray
That he would not talk
Because I would explode and he would be a dork
I held my breath, as he came near
After this I would probably need a beer
He opened his mouth
I screamed and I screamed
He shrank to the size of a mouse.

Heather Rogerson (10)
Fairholme Primary School, Feltham

Aliens

A n alien arrives on Earth to scare people,
L ittle aliens come too,
I nside the spaceship it is all green,
E verything is green even the aliens,
N othing is black or white.

Grace Rhodes (10)
Fairholme Primary School, Feltham

Trolls

A troll is very scary and very hairy.
A troll eats cats and rats.
A troll is very lazy and very crazy.
A troll is very grumpy and very lumpy.
A troll looked in his dish and granted a wish.
A troll went to bed and bumped his head.
A troll got a hen and found a pen.
A troll found a girl and did a whirl.

Megan Pugh (7)
Richmond First School, Sheerness

Grandad

He walks over fields
Even though old
Hours on end walking
For no purpose
Up steep hills
With his wife
A walking machine
He likes to talk
Telling stories
With meanings
You have to work out
Although interesting
He goes on forever
A talking machine
His chin
Is covered with a beard
As white as snow
His nose
As hairy as a shaggy dog
His hands
Wrinkled
And covered with veins
Rivers through his skin
His face
With fine lines
Like a marked ruler
He sits hunched in his chair
Reading an endless story
Sitting with his eyes fixed
On the page
A reading machine.

Josephine Whitehouse (9)
St Richards RC School, Chichester

Laughter

Laughter tastes like a big piece of air bursting into your mouth.
Laughter smells like a big fluffy marshmallow with ice cream on top.
Laughter looks like a big funny clown.
Laughter feels like a soft cosy cushion.
Laughter reminds me of France
When I laughed for ten minutes non-stop.

Robert Hutchings (9)
St Richards RC School, Chichester

Nanny

A bonfire which smokes
Enjoys the smoke running down her throat
Killing her every minute
She shops for the latest fashion
Pushing past to the front
So she won't be late for church.
Eating and scoffing food all the time.
She argues like a lawyer.
She demands to know what you have
Been doing in the past.
She's a hunter hungry for a walk
Around the canal.
Lapping everyone
She's like a speeding bullet.
When I was little
She held my hand.

James Li-Kam-Tin (9)
St Richards RC School, Chichester

Sadness

Sadness
It is a dark grey feeling,
It is a deafening sound,
If you are sad,
You will mourn and mourn and mourn,
Until the sadness lets you out of its grasp.

Sadness tastes like a crust of burnt bread,
Crumbling in your mouth,
The sickening taste gets greater.

Sadness smells like ashes burnt out,
Which once before was a blazing fire of love.

Elizabeth Whitehouse (9)
St Richards RC School, Chichester

Fear

Fear is grey and dark
Like a deserted cave,
A clashing sound
Like thunder.
It tastes like nothing,
A dry, empty mouth.
It smells chewy
Like goo.
It looks like a picture,
A picture of sadness.
It feels slithery
Like a snake.
It reminds me of
My worst nightmare.

Jack Clark (9)
St Richards RC School, Chichester

Dad

Smoke on the water
As a guitar machine
Steve Morse plucks
The guitar
And Ian Gillen voice
Flying in the air
And Dad sings
The words of
Smoke on the water.

Cameron Forrester (9)
St Richards RC School, Chichester

If I Had Wings

If I had wings
I would search for people I know
Like an eagle catching its prey.

If I had wings
I would visit the people on the Earth
And feel what no gravity feels like.

If I had wings
I would speed around
Like a Ferrari on a racetrack.

If I had wings
I would glide over countries
Like a plane carrying passengers over on holidays.

If I had wings
I would fly over the tallest tower
As tall as the sky.

Harry Li-Kam-Tin (9)
St Richards RC School, Chichester

My Brother Jack

He sits in his room
playing computer games
just sits there
with his dark brown shaggy hair
swaying slightly as his round sphere head moves
his tanned hand rests gently on the mouse
fingers move up and down
and a small clicking noise as the mouse squeaks
his knees gently bounce
for there are springs attached to his body
he mutters to himself, 'Got to win'
and he always calls me 'Old Bean'.

Megan Ekinsmyth (9)
St Richards RC School, Chichester

Anger

Anger is dark red
Anger is the core of the world

Anger sounds like lava gushing down a mountain
As if it is a waterfall

Anger tastes like red-hot chilli peppers
Burning your mouth

Anger smells like smoke
As if a forest fire is burning

Anger looks like burning sun
Squirting out some fire

Anger feels like fire
Burning someone's hand

Anger reminds me of volcanoes
Erupting down the hill.

Toby Henshaw (9)
St Richards RC School, Chichester

Tom

He sits slouched in his chair
Like a question mark
In his favourite place
Playing on the computer
His kind brown eyes stay focused on the screen
His hands are whizzing on the keys
A human typing machine
This is his favourite thing
He then gets up and does a silly dance
And then an impression of a well-known man
Then picks me up and twirls me around
His bedroom's a tip
We once found a gone-off cucumber in it
And a jar of mayonnaise
He gets out his Beanos every night
And his model aeroplane
But when it comes to eating
He refuses to eat his greens
Then plays with me
And calls me 'Hopping Mad'.

Hope Begley (9)
St Richards RC School, Chichester

Mum

Cycling to the shops
Listening to music
Bumping into people
Chatting like a chatterbox
Reading miles of words
Eyes light as the burning sun
Hair darker than dark.

Owen Haywood (9)
St Richards RC School, Chichester

Love

Love, the colour of pure gold,
as gold as a swift eagle.

Love, the noise of a bird when the day begins,
as quiet and as gentle as the sky.

Love, the taste of the sweetest recipe,
made by the best cook in the world.

Love, the smell of grass when it's been raining,
the smell of the sweetest perfume.

Love, it looks like the magic of a shooting star,
the small white feathers of a dove.

Love, it feels like a soft cloth,
softer than the clouds.

Love, reminds you of how you came to be here,
stepping on the small crust of the Earth.

Jack Oldroyd (9)
St Richards RC School, Chichester

If I Had Wings

If I had wings
I would touch the clouds up high
The softness like fluffy sheep.

If I had wings
I would storm through the sky
Where the wind is hard.

If I had wings
I would slice a piece of the sun
As hot as red-hot curry.

If I had wings
I would swim in the deep blue sea
High diving from the clouds.

If I had wings
I would drink the raindrops
Refreshing as spring.

Joseph Hellyer (9)
St Richards RC School, Chichester

Rain

I like it when it rains a lot,
All gushing down the drainpipes,
When puddles turn to oceans,
Loads of water in the streets,
It looks like it will never stop,
Rattling on the rooftops,
All of the heavens open
And it fills my world with joy.

James Gibson (9)
St Richards RC School, Chichester

Love

Love sounds like someone's heart pounding
fast as the time goes past.
Every day and night you think of that special someone
and their heartbeat.

Love tastes like yummy strawberries, juicy and red,
picking them off trees and eating them in bed.

Love smells like my mum's perfume
on a sunny day with no fumes.

Love looks like the girl of your dreams
in your arms in the hot water spar.

Love feels like your favourite chocolates, tender and smooth,
nice to eat when you're in the mood.

Love reminds me of sitting in bed
cuddling my favourite ted.

Kieran Miller (9)
Stafford Junior School, Eastbourne

Scared - A Cinquain

Gloomy.
Staring shadows.
All around my bedroom.
Frightening darkness all around me.
I'm scared!

Georgia Bellett (7)
Stafford Junior School, Eastbourne

My Fear Poem

Fear sounds like floorboards creaking.
Fear tastes like blood dripping from a dead body.
Fear smells like rotting dead animals.
Fear looks like spiders fighting for their lives.
Fear feels like some dead animal sliding down the back
of your neck.

Nathan Fuller (10)
Stafford Junior School, Eastbourne

Fear

Fear sounds like somebody frightened
Fear tastes like live fire in your house
Fear smells like somebody not feeling very well
Fear looks like somebody shivering
Fear feels like twinkling
Fear reminds you of somebody trying to catch me.

Lily Crossley (9)
Stafford Junior School, Eastbourne

Hate

Hate is when you're annoyed like burnt toast on fire.
It feels like something you don't want to give away but have to.
Hate is when you have been sent to bed early.
It looks like fire in a really hot oven.
It tastes like Brussels sprouts with extra vinegar on top.
It reminds me of war and killing people.

Christopher Daniels (10)
Stafford Junior School, Eastbourne

Darkness

Darkness is black like Simon Cowell's hair.
It sounds like a steam train coming out of a dark tunnel.
It tastes like a fervent potato that has just come out of the oven.
It smells like an intense burning forest.
Darkness feels like a black leather sofa.
It reminds me of my first day at school.

Zoe Heather (9)
Stafford Junior School, Eastbourne

Love

Love is orangy-red like a glowing sunset.
It sounds like a bird tweeting happily and cheerfully.
It tastes like biting into a juicy, crunchy sweet apple.
It smells like a bunch of red roses.
It feels like a big, fluffy, squidgy, soft cushion.
It reminds me of a dog having a small, cute, fluffy puppy.

Louise Grafham (10)
Stafford Junior School, Eastbourne

Hate

Hate is black like plague murdering the skin.
I think it tastes like a chicken gravy cube.
Hate smells like a shelter blazing down to the Earth.
It feels like a brick falling on my toe.
Hate reminds me of when my cat died.
Hate sounds like a witch cackling around her fizzing,
overflowing cauldron.

Laurence Cox (9)
Stafford Junior School, Eastbourne

Fear

Fear is white like a sharp and spiky shark's tooth.
Fear sounds like a girl awakening from the most horrific nightmare.
Fear tastes like microwaved but freezing spaghetti.
Fear feels like a drenched dog just in from the gushing rain.
Fear smells like the smelliest of all spices.
Fear reminds me of a screeching child.

Rachael Berrisford (9)
Stafford Junior School, Eastbourne

Darkness

Darkness is black like Simon Cowell's locks.
It sounds like a tempted angry rhino.
It smells like my mum's cooking of spaghetti.
It tastes like burnt bananas.
Darkness feels like I have not got any bravery at all.
It reminds me of my first day at school.

Caitlin Taylor Hood (10)
Stafford Junior School, Eastbourne

Witches

Witches are black like darkness in a haunted house.
They sound like pure evil cackling over a cauldron.
They taste like sour, slimy, toxic potions,
They smell like old snails, frogs and toads that they make
poisons with,
They remind me of walking into a haunted manor full of black magic,
They feel like warty lumps on evil mixed with slimy,
crumpled wrinkles.

Holly Ayres (9)
Stafford Junior School, Eastbourne

Laughter

Laughter is yellow like the sun's rays spreading warmth all around.
Laughter sounds like sleigh bells tinkling through the snow.
Laughter tastes like shimmering soda on the tip of my tongue.
Laughter smells like hot, saucy pepper teasing a sneeze.
Laughter feels like tinkling hands tinkling toes.
Laughter reminds me of the last day of school.

Demi-Jade Goodison (9)
Stafford Junior School, Eastbourne

Happiness

Happiness is rainbow-coloured like all the glowing colours,
It sounds like a massive bar of chocolate.
It smells like a perfume bottle.
It feels like there is nothing there apart from air.
It reminds me of a bright, colourful, printed wall.

Chloë Funnell (9)
Stafford Junior School, Eastbourne

Laughter

Laughter is like a rainbow, a coloured upside down smile.
Laughter is the sound of a magpie chuckling in his tree.
Laughter tastes like trying to talk with a gobstopper in my mouth.
Laughter smells like barbecue ribs hot from the oven ready to eat.
Laughter feels like being tickled by the most enormous
                                        ostrich feather.
Laughter reminds me of getting toys as special rewards
                                        when I'm good.

Daniel Wright (9)
Stafford Junior School, Eastbourne

Love

Love is pinky-red like a sunset on the beach,
It sounds like sparkling from a wishing star,
It tastes like fairy cakes, leaping around my tongue,
It smells like strawberry juice, sweet and red,
It feels like an arrow from Cupid, made in Heaven, warming my heart,
It reminds me of fire on a cold, unforgiving winter's day warming
my heart.

Rowan Fitzgerald (10)
Stafford Junior School, Eastbourne

Hate

Hate is black like death.
It sounds like a person scratching on a blackboard really loud
with long fingernails.
It tastes like lumpy burning food on my tongue.
It smells like a burning house on a rumbling fire.
It feels like a brick falling down on my toe repeatedly.
It reminds me of my first day at school.

Rosie Pugh (9)
Stafford Junior School, Eastbourne

Laughter

Laughter is multicoloured like a clown with his fluffy pink pompoms.
Laughter sounds like stars twinkling in the midnight air.
Laughter tastes like lots of sugary sweets.
Laughter smells like ice lollies dripping in my hand.
Laughter feels like red jelly wobbling in my hand.
Laughter reminds me of the bells on a Tudor jester's hat.

Marco Belim (9)
Stafford Junior School, Eastbourne

Laughter

Laughter is all the colours of the rainbow
like a clown's multicoloured enormous boots.
Laughter sounds like someone telling people gags.
Laughter tastes like lots of candy with assorted tastes.
Laughter smells like a sweet ice lolly dripping in my hand.
Laughter feels like slimy goo squishing in my hand.
Laughter reminds me of children having fun playing with their toys.

Jessica Weston (9)
Stafford Junior School, Eastbourne

Love

Love is a tropical colour and is like the sunset
It sounds like Valentine songs to my ears
It tastes like a tender steak, *mmm*
It smells like a rose shooting up in the yard
It feels like a butterfly flying
It reminds me of beauty and peace.

Jordan Ticehurst (9)
Stafford Junior School, Eastbourne

Fear

Fear is like a wolf whining at night,
Fear sounds like a blood-sucking scream,
Fear tastes like darkness and hatred,
Fear smells like plastic blazing on a fire,
Fear feels like an earthquake inside my tummy,
Fear reminds me of the Devil himself.

Lucas Belim (9)
Stafford Junior School, Eastbourne

Fear

Anger as a steam train rushing fast as lightning.
It sounds like a man who just got shot by a gun.
It tastes like a pie burnt in the oven.
It feels like a man who has a gun.
It feels like a train has just run you over nine times.
And it reminds me of when I went into the hospital.

Connor Baxter (9)
Stafford Junior School, Eastbourne

Hate

Hate is black like my first day at school.
It sounds like the teacher screaming when she's outside.
It tastes like black burning sausages.
It smells like a smelly tunnel with dirty water running down.
It feels like people cuddling me.
It reminds me that a person has just died.

Jude Kean (9)
Stafford Junior School, Eastbourne

Hate

Hate is black like my first day at school.
It sounds like the teacher scratching chalk down the blackboard.
It tastes like the black curly liquorice.
It smells like burning food in a kitchen.
It reminds me of death.

Samantha Irons (9)
Stafford Junior School, Eastbourne

Fear

Fear is black
Like a very dark forest
Sounds of an owl and scary music
It tastes of sprouts
It smells of rainwater on the leaves
It looks like an inky pen
It feels like prickles down your back.

Oliver Zecchin (10)
Stafford Junior School, Eastbourne

Silence

Silence is a mouse crawling around,
Silence is a whisper with no sound,
Silence of peace, death and harmony,
Silence is nothing at all really.

Danni Lewis (10)
Stafford Junior School, Eastbourne

Hate

Hate is pitch-black like a haunted ghost train struggling to get out.
It sounds like a witch wailing around her frothing, gurgling cauldron.
It tastes like disgusting Brussels sprouts boiling, cooked by the Devil.
It smells like dead people rising from the graveyard.
It feels like a humungous spider crawling all over me.
It reminds me of gruesome death!

Gemma Courtney-Davies (9)
Stafford Junior School, Eastbourne

The Day My Life Ended

There I was just staring out into space,
A man crept up behind me,
We were face to face.
With a black mask on
And a crowbar in his hand,
He hit my head, I fell to the ground.

Jamie Hill (10)
Stafford Junior School, Eastbourne

Love

Love is like strawberry flavoured cake on a Sunday afternoon.
Love is when you go out for a romantic dinner at noon.
Love is when he calls you up from work just to say hello.
Love is when he gives you some flowers and they all go peepo.
Love is something some might not understand.
Love is confusing and might fling out like an elastic band.
Love is in the world all around.

Taelor Roberson (10)
Stafford Junior School, Eastbourne

Anger

A nger is the fire which starts a volcano
N othing gets in its way
G etting hotter and redder, raring to go
E verybody running from the fiery mountain
R aging down the mountainside towards innocent people
whose lives will soon be lost.

Ben Cooper (10)
Stafford Junior School, Eastbourne

Love

Love is pink like candyfloss
Looks like a pink fluffy sheep
Sounds like a harp, soft and flowing
Love feels like a lovely soft pillow
Smells like a petal from a rose
It reminds me of pink confetti
And it tastes like strawberry chocolate.

Eleanor Grant (10)
Stafford Junior School, Eastbourne

Fear

The spookiness of the middle of the night
The howling of the night
When you walked into the graveyard
The sound of silence
And the gate squeaking behind you
Creepy headstones everywhere
Walking through the sound of mummies
Hearing in your head, screaming
Hearing ghosts and seeing them
Lying frightened
Locked in the graveyard.

Samantha May Avard (10)
Stafford Junior School, Eastbourne

Darkness

Darkness sounds like there's nobody with you.
Darkness tastes like somebody watching you in the dark,
growling night.
Darkness smells like you're in your room with your darkest fears.
Darkness looks like you're lost in outer space.
Darkness feels like nobody likes you and you're on your own.
Darkness reminds me of all my dead animals.

Charlie Mackay (8)
Stafford Junior School, Eastbourne

Silence

The dark and dull
High towering walls coming closer
Butterflies in your tummy
But the littlest sound
The clock ticking
Tick-tock, tick-tock
But that sound is no match for silence
The grandfather clock
Dinging and donging for midnight
Then there is the knocking sound under the floorboard
There is no more silence
Argh!

Benjamin Horan (10)
Stafford Junior School, Eastbourne

Fear

The fear ripped out my heart
It was like the spicy taste
Of red-hot chilli peppers
Burning down my throat
It looked like a scary dragon
And felt painful
Like me boiling in lava
I screeched as he grabbed me
His hot slimy hands
Felt icy like winter
And then that was it
I was gone.

Charley Baxter (10)
Stafford Junior School, Eastbourne

Laughter!

Laughter sounds like people laughing in the playground
Laughter smells like melted chocolate
Laughter looks like a smiley face
Laughter feels like someone whispering and laughing at you
Laughter tastes like fizzy Coke.

Roxanne Passmore (10)
Stafford Junior School, Eastbourne

Hunger

Hunger sounds like a rumbling in your tummy
Hunger tastes like crispy chicken
Hunger smells like steak with juicy lemon
Hunger looks like sausages wrapped round with sizzling bacon
Hunger feels like chocolate fudge cake
Hunger reminds me of roast lamb and mint sauce.

Benito Caira (10)
Stafford Junior School, Eastbourne

Laughter

Laughter sounds like having a good time at the park
Laughter tastes like chocolate ice cream with sauce running down
Laughter smells like popcorn popping in the pan
Laughter looks like having fun at a funfair
Laughter feels like happy feeling watching 'Tom and Jerry'
Laughter reminds me of being tickled by my mum and dad.

Jordan Curling (9)
Stafford Junior School, Eastbourne

Fear

Fear is like an ice cube running down your back
Fear is like a shiver of pain and death
Fear is like a ghost creeping up to you
Fear is like visiting a graveyard in the middle of the night
Fear is like the taste of flesh and bone
Fear is like the awakening of the dead
Fear is a flash of lightning
Fear is your worst nightmare
Fear is like a revolting thing to eat
Fear is a scream of terror and sadness
Fear is something that makes a tear run down your face
Fear is the sound of a thousand bombs hitting the ground
Fear is the sound of violins playing scary noises
Fear is the sound of a zombie coming near you
Fear is the sound of . . .

Charlotte Henderson (9)
Stafford Junior School, Eastbourne

Love

Love reminds me of my family and friends snuggling me
under my comfy bed.
Love looks like a sunny duet day.
Love tastes of strawberries with cream and sugar on.
Love smells of coconuts dripping and melting from the trees.
Love feels like touching the softest sponge in the world.
Love sounds like a lovely bit of talented music.

Hannah King (9)
Stafford Junior School, Eastbourne

Laughter

Laughter is happiness all around the world and hilarity in people.
It sounds like people excited, under the waving branches of the trees.
It tastes like mushrooms in the wild.
It smells like a family having a barbecue.
It looks like a baby cub with its mum having fun.
It feels as soft as a lion's fur.
It reminds you of your friend being funny to you.

Bradley Wainwright (10)
Stafford Junior School, Eastbourne

Hate!

Hate sounds like a bomb hitting a house
Hate tastes like mushy peas all green and sloppy
Hate smells like a house on fire
Hate looks like a sofa in the side of the road
Hate feels like someone dying
Hate reminds me of my brother annoying me all the time.

Chloe Oliver (9)
Stafford Junior School, Eastbourne

Laughter

Laughter sounds like children having fun and having a fabulous time
Laughter tastes like a hamburger just coming out the oven
                              ready to eat
It smells like a lovely baby that's just been born
It looks like children winning a tournament of basketball
Laughter's like the sun on a summer's day, gleaming in the sky
It reminds me of the brilliant times I have with my friends.
What about you?

Amber Earley (9)
Stafford Junior School, Eastbourne

Laughter

Laughter sounds like people going on holiday.
Laughter tastes of yummy sweets.
Laughter smells like toasted waffles.
Laughter looks like children playing football.
Laughter feels like your heart is pumping and pumping.
Laughter reminds me of *Arsenal* playing football.

Charles Truman (9)
Stafford Junior School, Eastbourne

Love

Love looks like flowers and animals, dancing on a lovely spring day.
Love sounds like birds tweeting in a tree.
Love is what connects you with your family and friends and pets.
Love is shaped like love hearts and a rainbow, combined to make
a rainbow made out of love hearts.
Love is a feeling that everyone has.
Love tastes like chocolate given by your mum.
Love feels like you, snug as a bug in your bed.
Love reminds me of Christmas and a newborn child on a spring day.

Oscar Griffiths (10)
Stafford Junior School, Eastbourne

Hate!

Hate is when you dislike something that you can't dislike anymore!
If someone says, 'I hate you,' it leaves an icy chill up your spine.
It smells like Marmite, yucky and strong.
It reminds me of an explosion in my mind.
It feels like puke, gross all over the ground.
It sounds like the sting of an electric eel.
Hate tastes like a plate full of cowpat.
It looks like somebody having their head chopped off.
But let's just put it this way, hate is not a nice thing.

Rio Ashcroft (9)
Stafford Junior School, Eastbourne

Fear

Fear is like a cold, damp alleyway, filled with a wisp of mist
and no light.
Fear is a cold winter's night, with ghostly shadows, crystal and frost.
Fear is a murderer on the loose, hungry for fresh blood.
Fear is a ghostly nightmare, enough to chill the bone marrow.
Fear is flesh and bone and battle, a thing never long gone.
Fear is a thing prowling graveyards, littered with hollow bones.
Fear is something behind you, a scabbed hand of a stranger.
Fear is something of a person's death, a thing to make tears fall.
Fear is a scream of mercy and pleading, a scream that shakes
the Earth.
Fear is a thunderstorm, engulfing the Earth in its mighty hands.
Fear is the birth of evil, flowering into a terrible bloom.
Fear is a girl huddled in the corner of the room, not knowing
what will happen next.
Fear is all these things but most of all . . .
It's behind you!

Eric Barrell (9)
Stafford Junior School, Eastbourne

Darkness

Darkness sounds like a feather falling,
I can hear my telephone calling.
Darkness tastes like mint hot chocolate,
sometimes you can smell fire in the air.
Darkness looks like a burnt roast dinner.
It feels like you're walking through a deep dark tunnel.
Darkness reminds me of being wrapped up in my quilt in my bed.

Julia Griffin (9)
Stafford Junior School, Eastbourne

Darkness

Darkness sounds like the howl of the night.
Darkness tastes as nice as a hot drink.
Darkness smells like smoke from a bonfire.
Darkness looks like my bedroom at night.
Darkness feels like someone's watching me.
Darkness reminds me of dark caves.

Elliott Curryer (9)
Stafford Junior School, Eastbourne

Darkness

Darkness sounds like an echo coming from a tunnel
Darkness tastes like a lemon sherbet
Darkness smells like wood from a tree
Darkness looks like a black hole
Darkness feels like a nightmare
Darkness reminds me of a graveyard.

Abbie Johnson (9)
Stafford Junior School, Eastbourne

Darkness

Darkness sounds like the silence of a cemetery
but the leaves rustling.
Darkness tastes like something bitter, like chewing gum
that's lost its flavour.
Darkness feels like something cold and hard.
Darkness smells like a wire burning.
Darkness looks like something that's creeping slowly up to you,
its feet tapping - *tap, tap, tap, tap.*
Darkness reminds you of a leaking pipe with water dripping
on your shoulder that causes you to tremble and shiver -
drip, drip, drip.
That's what I call darkness.

Alice Marshall (9)
Stafford Junior School, Eastbourne

Laughter

Laughter sounds like a Christmas bell, *jingle, jingle*.
Laughter tastes like a seafront shell.
It smells like sausage drifting through the air.
Laughter looks like happy families.
Laughter feels like the vibration of a cup.
It reminds me of Christmas day when the newborn king came.

Nathan Stoddern-Deery (9)
Stafford Junior School, Eastbourne

The Bandstand

Bandstand
I like watching
Mummy is in the band
Toot, toot, toot goes the flugel horn
Listen.

Tegan Inch (7)
Stafford Junior School, Eastbourne

Tongue Twister

Tall teddy had a terrific tall tower.
Terrific teddy had a tall trumpet.
Teddy's teacher told Ted off for telling tales.

Bayley Grant (7)
Stafford Junior School, Eastbourne

Crafty Cat

Crafty cat crouched on the couch.
Crawling, creeping, crafty cat.
Curled up crafty cat crouched cosily in the cot.

Ronnie Parks (7)
Stafford Junior School, Eastbourne

Happy - A Cinquain

Happy.
I am smiling.
Very happy today.
My holiday is nearly here.
Hooray!

Charlie King (7)
Stafford Junior School, Eastbourne

Anger

Anger is red like lava tumbling down the mountains,
Screams and shouts crashing through your ears,
Hot chilli peppers sizzling sharply down your throat,
Sniffing the ash left from a fire,
The dragon's mouth filled with red burning flames,
Feels like a sunburn so sharp and spicy feelings across your neck,
Reminds you that you're out of control and colourful.

Sam Haffenden (10)
Stafford Junior School, Eastbourne

Danger

Danger is the colour black, all dark and scary.
The sound of danger is someone being murdered.
A sour sweet is the taste of danger.
The smell of fear is all around.
Looks all empty, worried and frightened.
Feels like someone under your bed.
Reminds you of a scary movie you saw on telly.

Josie Pollard (10)
Stafford Junior School, Eastbourne

Darkness

D arkness! It's cold and wet,
A ll night long it's there,
R ustling and moving, you're scared to death,
K ing of the night!
N ever is it tired,
E very night you see it! Not light,
S cared stiff in your bed,
S o when you wake up, make sure it's light.

Rosie Reeves (10)
Stafford Junior School, Eastbourne

Billie Is Coming Over

Billie
Billie's coming
Billie is my best friend
Billie's coming over to sleep
Billie!

Ellie Paine (8)
Stafford Junior School, Eastbourne

Waves

Crash, crash
Rough waves crashing
Washing mussels away
Suck, suck, sucking the cold water
Crash, crash.

William Nicholls (7)
Stafford Junior School, Eastbourne

My House

My house
It's cool my house
My house's cosy and warm
My house's cosy, warm and
Welcoming
My house.

Lorcan Taylor-Hood (7)
Stafford Junior School, Eastbourne

Stafford - Cinquain

Stafford
Is the best school
My friends go to Stafford
I have school dinners every day
Best school!

Megan Haines (8)
Stafford Junior School, Eastbourne

Princess (My Dog) - Cinquain

My dog
is black and white.
She chases rabbits and
eats dry dog food and she likes it.
Go girl!

Charlotte Tester (7)
Stafford Junior School, Eastbourne

Come And See The Shape I'm In

Tall as an elephant
Thin as a ruler
Wide as a bridge
Bright as the sun
I'm sometimes this
And sometimes that
But I'm never ever funny or fat.

Aimee Gray (7)
Stafford Junior School, Eastbourne

My Mum And Dad And Me - A Cinquain

Hugging.
Hugging a lot.
Playing with my sisters.
Playing with my mum and my dad.
So good.

Rebekah Hadland (7)
Stafford Junior School, Eastbourne

Love

Love is the colour pink all fluffy and cute,
Love sounds like Cupid playing his harp,
Love looks like pink fluffy sheep grazing peacefully,
Love tastes like strawberry milk,
Love feels like my mum and dad's hugs,
Love smells like the sweet smell of flowers,
Love reminds me of my family.

Chloe Monks (10)
Stafford Junior School, Eastbourne

Laughter

Laughter is like orange flavoured jelly, wobbling in your belly.
Laughter sounds like Tigger bouncing around - *boing, boing, boing.*
Laughter tastes like orange cake on a Sunday morning.
Laughter feels like being silly.
Laughter looks like people moving their lips,
Laughter smells like people having fun.

Ryan Jenner (10)
Stafford Junior School, Eastbourne

Love

Love is pink like candyfloss swirling on a stick,
Sounds like a harp, soft and floaty with caramel so tasty to eat,
Wedding bells are ringing with pink confetti so sweet,
It looks like pink fluffy sheep,
Smells like a petal from a pink rose
And feels like a fluffy heart cushion,
Love is very shiny.

Georgia Tree (10)
Stafford Junior School, Eastbourne

Anger!

Anger is red like hot bubbling lava.
It sounds like a screaming kettle.
It tastes like a green poison leaf.
It smells like burnt ebony.
It reminds me of a black demon coming for your red blood.
It feels like your head is coming off from an explosion.

Edward Discombe (11)
Stafford Junior School, Eastbourne

Anger

Lava bubbling up in a volcano
Hot steam rising in the air
Hot chilli peppers burning in your mouth
A dragon breathing fire
Ashes going everywhere.

Callum Smith (10)
Stafford Junior School, Eastbourne

Love

Love is pink like candyfloss floating and swirling.
Love smells like beautiful petal perfume.
Love tastes like the sensations of strawberries.
Love reminds me of my mum giving me her love.
Love feels like fluffy pink sheep.
Love looks like a lake of love.
Love sounds like a harp being played at sunset on the beach.

Ceri Shields (10)
Stafford Junior School, Eastbourne

Darkness

Darkness is black like a monster's pounding heart.
Darkness sounds like a dead man's cracking bones.
Darkness tastes like a Homo sapien's blood spilling from
a wounded hand.
Darkness smells like the howling wind blowing against your face.
Darkness feels like a creepy figure stalking you.
Darkness reminds me of the black sky at night.

Hayden Oakleigh (10)
Stafford Junior School, Eastbourne

Hunger

Hunger is like someone dancing in my tummy.
Hunger sounds like the rustling trees.
Hunger tastes like a bitter taste.
Hunger smells like thin air.
Hunger feels like an empty void in your belly.
Hunger reminds me of the cold winter's night.

Lee Tudor (10)
Stafford Junior School, Eastbourne

Fear

Fear is black like the sky at night,
It sounds like silence in an abandoned graveyard.
Fear tastes like a rotten man's bones,
It smells like smoke from a bonfire.
Fear feels like someone in a boat cascading off a cliff
And reminds me of being stalked through a gloomy wood.

Oliver Loades (11)
Stafford Junior School, Eastbourne

Anger

Anger is red like a volcano about to explode
Anger sounds like a howling wolf, *worr*
Anger tastes like chilli burning in my mouth
Anger smells like socks lying on the bed
Anger feels like ghosts flying through the wind
Anger reminds me of just sitting and reading a book.

Yasmin Morgan (10)
Stafford Junior School, Eastbourne

Fear

Fear is white, as the swirling Atlantic Ocean,
It sounds like a creeping mouse under the floorboards,
It tastes like a frozen ice cube slipping down my throat
It smells like a mouldy tomato on a sunny afternoon,
It feels like a spider crawling down my back and arms
It reminds me of ghosts in an abandoned castle.

Isaac Betts (10)
Stafford Junior School, Eastbourne

Love

Love is light red, leaking out of a heart,
Love sounds like a heartbeat, *boom, boom!*
Love tastes like a gummy bear in-between your teeth.
Love smells like a strawberry moose creeping up your nose,
Love feels like smooth bubble bath up against your body,
Love reminds me of red coloured petals, massaging your feet.

Luke Brett (10)
Stafford Junior School, Eastbourne

Hunger

Hunger is grey like an empty feeling in your tummy,
Hunger sounds like a tiny voice wishing in your belly,
Hunger tastes like the odour of apple pie baking in the oven.
Hunger smells like lasagne swelling up in the oven,
Hunger feels like a washing machine rumbling in your belly,
It reminds me of dreaming about ice cream and cherries
Slithering down my throat.

Sam Bowles (10)
Stafford Junior School, Eastbourne

Love

Love is pink like a flamingo's feather,
It sounds as beautiful as a blackbird's song.
As tasty as a cloud of candyfloss.
Love smells like perfume, a lily or rose,
Love looks like a hug or a kiss from someone you love.
Love feels like a hug or a big fluffy pillow,
Love reminds you of the warmth of your mother's arms.
It's more beautiful than a ballet dancer, twirling around a dance floor,
But not quite as luscious as it seems,
It can hurt you more deeply than a slash in the head,
But don't let it destroy your hopes or your dreams.

Elizabeth Pipe (10)
Stafford Junior School, Eastbourne

Love

Love is rosy red, like a bird chanting in the morning,
It sounds like gentle trees echoing in the wind.
It tastes like lovely ice cream sliding down your throat,
It smells like roses swaying under your nose,
It feels like ruby cherries all delicate and round,
It reminds me of chocolate, all hot and melted.

Jack Burdon (10)
Stafford Junior School, Eastbourne

Love

Love is red like a heart beating at night
Sounds of romance colourful
As beautiful as a rose blooming in the sun
Soft like a love bear sitting on your bed
Love is as sweet as eating chocolate.

Ben Davis (10)
Stafford Junior School, Eastbourne

Love

Love is red like a heart
And a sound of romance,
Love is beautiful like Miss Webb and Mrs Tutt,
Love can get ugly sometimes,
Or it can get more softer, like a teddy bear.

Joshua Curling (10)
Stafford Junior School, Eastbourne

Love

Love is shades of red and pink
like fires crackling and burning,
it sounds as calm as when
a school choir sings.
As tasty as lumps of candyfloss,
love smells of flowers and as sweet
as a juicy fruit salad.
It looks like roses and it fills
you with joy.
Love makes you feel safe and warm,
it's something that will stay with you forever.
It's adorable, like your favourite bear.
Love is something everyone needs and
it makes you feel full inside!

Lorna Bonwick (10)
Stafford Junior School, Eastbourne

Love

Love is romance like a flower,
Love can be like a lemon, very sour.
Love is for always, never break up,
Love can be scary but they stay in their cup.
Love is sweet for all the couples,
But they always stay close, like buckles.

Chloe Beadsworth (10)
Stafford Junior School, Eastbourne

Fear

Fear is black like Dracula's cloak,
Screaming is heard when you are scared,
Tasting like poison.
Fear smells of old, crunchy leaves in a graveyard,
It looks like lightning in the sky,
Fear feels like being at funerals,
You are reminded of all the scary moments in life.

Danu Hadden-Eccles (10)
Stafford Junior School, Eastbourne

Laughter

Laughter is yellow like a broad beaming smile,
It is the thing that makes you happy when you are sad.
Laughter is joy and happiness mixed up to be one,
The feeling of laughter is warm and cuddly,
Laughter tastes like sweet candy,
You are reminded of all the good times.

Ellie Carden (10)
Stafford Junior School, Eastbourne

Peace At Last

Eternal sleep now passed
Drowsily I awakened
A loud bump made me start
Sudden and with a jump
My tail recurled to return
To the land of dreams I drift
Until an annoying thump, I do declare
The sound of thundering footsteps
Trenching above my head
The spell of the roof pulls me in
The cat flap, flaps vigorously
As I claw my way up the tree
At last I reached the branches
After prowling up the trunk
A troublesome squirrel nibbled a nut
I spat, hissed then pounced
The pesky creature scrambled away
And a good thing too
At last I found peace
Curled up and purring, I sleep.

Marina West (10)
Thomas's Battersea, London

The Journey Through Sunrise

Gloomily I awoke,
The starless night was gone
The sun rose high
Kissing the morning sky
The dazzling bird of paradise
Sailed the morning by.

Alexia Mavroleon (9)
Thomas's Battersea, London

Winter Poem

Skaters glide smoothly
Scarves flap wildly
Trees stand bare
On a cold winter's day

Children stir coins into Christmas pudding.
Radiators hum soothingly
Squirrels run quickly
On a cold winter's day.

Christmas tree lights flicker merrily
Presents sleep dreamily
Log fires burn cosily
On a cold winter's day.

Snow drifts lazily
Bells ring faintly
Santa flies through the night
On a cold Christmas Eve.

Ivo Thomas (8)
Thomas's Battersea, London

Welcome Autumn

The wind whistling past my head,
Snowflakes landing on my tongue,
Cold air settling on my face,
Water dripping on my hair.

Children laughing happily,
Leaves crackling on the pavement,
Birds twittering loudly,
Hedgehogs snuffling eagerly.

The smells of crumble wafting through the countryside,
Damp leaves making a smell,
Puree, smelling sweet and yummy,
Apples rotting, smelling strangely.

Leaves dancing to the ground,
Making rainbows on the ground,
Bare trees, very cold,
Squirrels scampering wildly.

Joshua Hampson (8)
Thomas's Battersea, London

Autumn's Coming!

Fluffy grey squirrels prancing and skating round the trees
Swampy brown, burning orange and tinkling yellow leaves
Twirling and dancing like on its wedding day
Red cute robins, cheeping loudly
Mud squelching between your toes
Hedgehogs snuffling crazily at worms
Trees whooshing madly from side to side
Owls hooting wisely
Autumn's here!

Conner Wakeman (8)
Thomas's Battersea, London

Autumn's Back Again

The leaves crackle on the pavement,
the red and blue birds chirp in the trees.
The hedgehogs snuffle along and are
trying to find a place to hibernate.
The golden glittering leaves are
swaying down from the trees.
Cold wind whispering through the leaves,
the crispy sound of the blazing leaves
being dragged along.
The feeling of diving into crispy sunset-coloured leaves
and the crispness of the fresh cold wind.
Sounds of laughter and fun.
There are old leaves and new ones
changing colour overhead.
Crispy blue skies, misty mornings, wispy clouds
drifting lazily across the glittering skies.

Harry Mark (8)
Thomas's Battersea, London

Lesson Fever!

The teacher jumped around
And punched and kicked the wall.
Susan ran to her school bag
And got her disco ball.

Our teacher sang so loudly
It really hurt our ears,
She found a small microphone
And sang like Britney Spears!

The children clapped and cheered,
And waved their arms around.
My teacher grabbed Joe's hands
Then hurled him to the ground!

Robbie played some music,
The type of music was rock
And Emily joined the dancing
She pranced around in her smock.

A boy was going crazy
He waved at his friends with glee.
But then a boy's trousers fell down
And that boy was me. *Eeeeeeek!*

Katie Pitman (9)
Thomas's Battersea, London

Autumn

A nimals scuffling swiftly
U nder the ground hedgehogs prepare for winter
T hrilling leaves twirl to the ground gracefully
U ndergrowth dies away
M en shuffle leaves in the morning mist
N oses smelling apple pie.

Tom Howard (8)
Thomas's Battersea, London

Autumn Is Coming

Autumn is coming,
    soft and swiftly
        gliding and darting in the cold mists.

Hedgehogs snuffling,
    people snuggling in warm woolly jumpers,
        the yummy smell drifting through.

The glistening sky, twinkling brightly
    the leaves waltzing gracefully,
        down the huge trees.

The wind howling like vicious wolves,
    apples falling angrily against
        the hard grassy floor.

Deer fighting dangerously,
    their horns sharp and pointy,
        their eyes burning as red as fire!

Birds racing off quickly
    through the heavy landscape,
        journey ahead to the toasty south.

Freezing cold water
    swaying gently, side by side,
        soon to be still and glassy.

Georgina Farmer (8)
Thomas's Battersea, London

Leaves

Leaves twirl and whirl until they reach the ground
Leaves crackle on the ground while people walk by
Leaves dance on the trees and in the tree trunks
Brown ones, red ones, gold ones and yellow ones
falling gracefully
The wind blows softly while leaves rustle along the ground.

Hannah Coles (8)
Thomas's Battersea, London

Autumn

Shuffling, crackling
Golden yellow,
Fire red, caramel brown.
Children jumping in leaves having lots of fun.
People laughing.
Red robins twittering in the trees.
It smells like damp, crispy leaves.
Leaves cling to your damp wellies.
Autumn has come!
Autumn has come!

Rebecca Versteegh (8)
Thomas's Battersea, London

Winter

Winter is when it begins to snow
The fire in houses crackle and glow
In the winter, it is very cold
Put on warm clothes, I am told
It's so cold the lakes start to freeze
And people begin to cough and sneeze.

Alanna Scott (8)
Thomas's Battersea, London

The Journey Of The Seasons That Go On

The seasons change with the whispers of the wind.

Rusty coloured leaves crackle to the ground
like the sound of paper burning in the wooden fire.
The wind blows all the mahogany-coloured leaves up
like a dance in the autumn air.
Now autumn must go on.

Luscious grass shivers in the furious wind.
The enchanted trees dance around in the cool winter air.
Leaves fall like snowflakes to the mahogany carpet below.
Now winter must go by.

The sun rises like a face that never stops smiling.
The bare trees lay untouched like a secret hidden away.
The rainbow flowers burst out like shooting stars.
Now spring must go by.

The waves are so calm you can hear a blade of grass.
The sun comes out and warms the budded trees.
The sun hides half of the seasons behind it with joy.
Now summer must go by.

Hannah Burt (9)
Thomas's Battersea, London

Autumn

The trees shake as the wind blows
Leaves scatter across and flow,
Different shapes of leaves orange, yellow and green
Children run around excitedly.

It is getting colder and colder
Trees are going through a metamorphosis
Conkers begin to drop
Squirrels scamper around.

Birds swoop, looking for food
The wind's icy chill
Autumn is here
Thankfully, only once a year.

Bea Thirsk (8)
Thomas's Battersea, London

Hallowe'en

On the last day of October it's Hallowe'en
When people dress up to be seen.
In scary costumes
These people dress up
And go out at night.

The children are on the prowl for sweets
And some others are looking for treats
If you hear a knock
You might see some scary frocks
Witches, zombies and bats.

They go around the streets looking for doors
And when they get there
They look at you with hideous eyes peeking through their hair
And all you hear is . . .
'Trick or treat?'

Viola Lough (8)
Thomas's Battersea, London

The Journey Of A Snowball

Silence reigns in the glistening valley,
The only thing that can be heard is the sloshing of the snow.
One ball, two balls, three balls,
Have been added to the massive arsenal of silver balls!
Children hide behind snow ports,
Standing proud as soldiers.
One patient snowball, like all the others before it, waits,
Suddenly it's picked up and thrown with tremendous force.
Swooping majestically,
Whistling past a rainbow of brightly coloured hats.
The snowball yearns to hit its given target.
Unexpectedly, he struck home.
Soaking the thick wool jacket full and through,
Knocking its victim off its feet.
Once again, a snowball is thrown.
Target hit
And forgotten forever.

Gabriel Slaughter (9)
Thomas's Battersea, London

The Volcano In Fudgi

The lava boils like the sun,
It burns and makes bubbles of heat hotness,
It rises like the sun coming up,
And trying to burst out.

It spurts out and boils the stones as the meteors
Fliy down below,
As it explodes majestically like a bomb,
The lava is happy to touch the ground.

The lava crushes with speed,
It travels like sound down the hill.
Mysteriously and is happy to reach the first houses
And breaks them down to the ground.

The lava is ready to destruct the land,
It destroys the houses and the hotels,
Fudgi is gone, never again to be seen,
Only the ruins remain.

Maxi Frankel (9)
Thomas's Battersea, London

Snowflakes

The graceful snowflakes sparkled
in the blinding sun,
they danced to the blanket of snow delicately,
and landed softly.
Some more snowflakes fluttered to the ground,
melted into the blanket prettily landing softly
on top of the other ones.

All of the snowflakes melted into the
white crisp carpet,
like diamonds swirling preciously.
nothing could be heard except
the wailing wind.
Now the blanket was as full as a cloud.

The white carpet looked like a duvet cover
from a bed,
sparkling in the sunrays,
shimmering lightly.
The carpet looked like a crystal-clear frozen pond,
laying forgotten in the middle of the forest.

The grey murky clouds vanished,
no snowflakes were to be seen,
everything was white and glittery.
The sun shone brightly onto the Earth
and everything lit up.

Emmanuelle Moore (9)
Thomas's Battersea, London

The Journey Of A Butterfly

The gorgeous butterfly was once
A soft playful, squirmy caterpillar
Crawling about the land
Trying to find some food.

Next, the hanging insect waits patiently
For the caterpillar to crawl up the suspicious tree
And creep into the cocoon.

The cocoon's wish has come true
The fluffy caterpillar, slithered up the tree
Leaving a trail behind,
He crawled into the anxious bug and fell fast asleep.

Last but not least, the caterpillar jumps
Out of his cocoon
But he catches himself with his beautiful wings
And he can see the world from that height.

Olivia Lo Primo (9)
Thomas's Battersea, London

Smoke

As I carefully strode to the grey blanket
Everything turned blurry
Everything turned strange,
Forcing my eyes to close.

It swirled and curled around me,
Clogging up my lungs.
Swirling through my body,
Causing me to fade.

When I'm gone,
The smoke's job is done.
Then it disappears and is never seen again,
Now I'm gone, I'm gone forever.

Quentin Géczy (9)
Thomas's Battersea, London

The Terrible Storm

The grey clouds roll in like warhorses,
They're like a barrier against the sun.
The lightning strikes everything that gets in its way
While the thunder roars like a lion,
Overcoming every noise.

Gusts of wind come past like howling wolves,
The rain lashes down like bullets.
All the ships that dare to cross, get demolished
And torn to shreds.

The sun tries its hardest to get through
But the barrier is too hard to break
The waves crash together
Like a crate hitting the ground
At tremendous speed.

The storm finally starts to move off
The shipwrecks float around homeless
And lost in the deep
Finally the clouds go away and the
Sun shines once again.

Max Dear (9)
Thomas's Battersea, London

The Piglet

It was on the stroke of ten when he awoke,
He cried and mourned, for he was lost in the pitch-black.
His frostbitten tail tingled as he trotted around the frosty barn,
His feet thundered as he walked around, desperate for a way out.
There was a little hole, big enough for his tiny-weenie body.
He found himself in a wide-open country.
He journeyed over freezing lakes, frosty mountains
Stood in the distance, howling like hounds.
Suddenly there in front of him were rows and rows of pigs.
He was immediately confused and felt in glimmering paradise.

Alexander Hersov (10)
Thomas's Battersea, London

Raindrops

The sun sparkles to the Earth
As the clouds start to come out.
They glide easily toward the flaming
Fireball in the sky.
The sun starts to fade as the puffy clouds shadow them,
And then it starts.

The rain begins,
It looks as if glass is floating from the sky
To meet the cobbled ground.
Millions of original raindrops drift down,
It's a gorgeous sight.

A raindrop looks like a diamond,
It feels like a frozen needle,
It glistens and glitters in its own way.
Everything sparkles,

When all the raindrops vanish,
The clouds slide away,
And the beautiful sun comes out again.
Everyone smiles.

Savannah Murphy (9)
Thomas's Battersea, London

The Journey Of A Snowflake

The snowflake slips and slides out of the cloud
As it falls, it twirls in the sky like a ballet dancer.
It is dazzling, just like a diamond
The starry snowflake is swirling in the air.

When it falls, it gracefully falls, dancing in the air,
And the soft, silky snowflake twinkles in the sky.
The amazing colours gleam in the morning sunlight
The air is crisp and cold.

The snowflake is almost at the end of its journey
It can see the white fluffy carpet below.
As it edges towards the ground, it whistles
And lands smoothly with its friends on the crunchy ground.

Lauren Anderson (9)
Thomas's Battersea, London

The Journey Of A Droplet Of Water

The drop of water skis down the mountain,
Swishing and swirling as it goes,
It soars down and down till it reaches the rapids,
It suddenly halts, silent and still.

It then glides through the crystal-clear water,
And flies and soars through the air
Like an aeroplane reaching its destination.
It reaches the glistening water below.

It emerges into the shimmering water
And bounces back up like an acrobat.
The glassy water makes a splash
And the droplet finds its way back to the water.

The droplet swirls and twirls
Like a ballerina dancing and prancing around,
Suddenly the water becomes salty, it has reached
The end of its journey.

Ambrosia Hicks (9)
Thomas's Battersea, London

The Rat

It tumbles dramatically down the stinking tube
It squeaks, it cries in the horrible filth,
The sewer is a mini world.
For the rat, it's a green bath.
Will it survive?

The pipes in the sewer, twist and turn
Like a roller coaster ride,
The rat, ecstatic all that way,
Suddenly it plops out.
It is in a greater tunnel now but this
Doesn't twirl and swirl.
Will it survive?

Water gushes from all directions,
It swishes, it swirls, like a tsunami,
The rat is swept off its feet
Like a leaf in the wind.
Will it survive?

It sees a light filtering from above,
The rat is overjoyed.
It takes a giant leap like a superhero saving someone.
The hole is so small but it manages to fit in!
Will it survive?
Yes it does!

Christian Nourry (9)
Thomas's Battersea, London

The Ghostly Journal

The ghost swooped in the gloomy wind
Like a tormented dragon.
The misty clouds covered him
With a sudden spike of thunder.

You could hear sinister screams
From the eerie haunted house.
Bats fluttered from the turreted tower
As the ghost crept through the broken window.

His entrance caused havoc:
Gushing wind swept from room to room
Causing damage to all that lived inside.
Sudden silence broke through the walls.

From then on that sinister mansion was ruled
By the mighty master of ghosts.

Evan Langmuir (10)
Thomas's Battersea, London

The Journey Of A Waterfall

The glassy water glides down the mountain,
Like a snake slithering around the desert.
It gushes quietly as it rushes down.

It twists and turns, not knowing where to go,
It swirls and whirls through the shallow gorge.
The crystal-clear water is in sight below,
Frothing and shimmering in the light,
Waiting for it to come.

It flies down with a plunge
Into the shimmering pool,
Its reflection is gone now,
For it's on its way.

It swirls, winding its way through
Round the silver water.
It's through, into the shimmering sea,
It's gone and its journey is over.

Paulina Hoeller-Suleiman (9)
Thomas's Battersea, London

The Dolphin

The dolphin leaps out in an arch,
He plunges into the ocean
Leaving spray and white horses,
Trickling on the sea.

The deep coral world below
Filled with colours,
Pink, blue, red, green, orange, purple
Lay swiftly on the ground.

The reef flows
With clown fish and sardines
All dancing in the current,
The dolphin snatches his prey
And retreats once again.

The sunset's reflection shines
In the dolphin's beady eyes,
He dives beneath the inky ocean
And disappears for the night.

Emmanuelle Zaoui (9)
Thomas's Battersea, London

Through A Telescope

In the sky so high
Stars were twinkling brightly
Shooting stars from left to right
The clouds had departed
The moon had just come through
Stars making pretty pictures
And the moon smiled down
As the sun rose at dawn
Morning had broken.

Jewel Leanne Boothe (9)
Thomas's Battersea, London

Sunrise

She awakes from her cloudy bed,
Slowly she glides
Her pale rosy cloak
Expanding over the green belt of land.

Higher an higher she sails,
Golden hair streaming behind.

Leafy trees and emerald grass,
Salute her with open arms.
Happy to be once again
Whispering in her wake.

Higher and higher she sails,
Golden hair streaming behind.

Animals emerge from their lairs,
Dusky and damp like newborns.
They stretch their noses,
To be kissed by the warmth of her lips.

Higher and higher she sails,
Golden hair streaming behind.

As her gaze crosses the lake,
A thousand tiny waves leap with joy.
Their silver forelocks,
Tossed by the hem of her foamy gown.

Higher and higher she sails,
Golden hair streaming behind.

And finally the sky embraces her,
As her glowing face pierces the expanse.
They gladly join,
To start a new day.

James Murphy (9)
Thomas's Battersea, London

The Journey Of A Pirate

A ship sets sail from a blood-splattered port,
To pick up the meat that snorts and snorts.
They have a feast and then head east,
To raid and capture the vessels of the best.
While the cannons go boom and the riggings shake.
The boarding-plank is thrown by the Devil himself.
The black-hearted crew charge and yell
Screaming with the pain and the burning of the flame.
The Devil has won this bloodshed, he has won the hostages.
Along with the breathtaking jewels.

Oliver Johnson-Smith (9)
Thomas's Battersea, London

Eagle's Prey

The eagle can tell he is near,
For he has picked up the scent.
His eyes gleam as he spots his prey:
A colony of fish, swifter than the running stream.

Terror strikes the fishes,
Who would be next of their colony?
With the agility of a cat and the strength
Of a lion, the eagle strikes!

Fish scatter left and right
As the blood wraith helps settle his appetite.
Fishes that are lucky, cower behind the rocks and plants
To escape the hunger of an eagle.

Ethan Chen (9)
Thomas's Battersea, London

Autumn Travel

I gazed
A massive train revealed
The pain began
In my brain
Started the train

I saw
My life fast forward
The leaves falling
Conkers shining
Autumn crawling

I watched
The festivals run past
Roshashana, Hanukah
Sukkot, Yom Kipper
When the Jews fast

I stared
As the shimmering snow
Kissed my forehead
I felt fine
And my brain was fed.

Louis Elton (10)
Thomas's Battersea, London

The Coming Of Winter

Winter drapes her white frosty cape,
Over the leaf-covered ground.
Further she walks,
Covering everything in a cold blanket.
Nothing can escape from the lashing winds
That herald her rumoured arrival.

Bare trees chatter wildly,
Huddling together
For much needed warmth,
And suddenly she is upon them,
Nothing escapes,
No pond, no bird,
No brightly coloured flower,
All hide and wait
For spring to melt the tyrant
And reduce her dominant power.

Cassius Bandeen (9)
Thomas's Battersea, London

The Journey Of Wind

It dances and swishes
It does what it wishes,
It's blustery, it howls,
It can be quite foul.

It strokes the trees,
As the rustle in the breeze,
It swishes the leaves up
Into the shape of a cup.

The sky was so bright,
A blinding, flashing light,
Dancing around with great might.
What a wonderful sight.

On the doormat,
In the coldness I sat.
It was the end of the day
And soon it will be May.

The sun has gone down,
The darkness was brown,
But with little warning,
It soon will be morning.

Isabella Hindley (10)
Thomas's Battersea, London

The Car Journey

Skidding and sliding and almost colliding
Galloping in the luminous night
Passing the meadow without a soul bare
Come to a glittery lake
Moonlit from the bright moon
Trees dangling into the water
Raindrops falling into the depths
And ripples going on and on like an immortal life.

Fast approaching a tunnel, an arch
Sounds echoing - *drip drop*
A screech could be heard
Tearing your ears, like a bat screeching for life
Or a mythological creature

At the end of the tunnel!

Sam Meeson-Frizelle (9)
Thomas's Battersea, London

The Journey

It's different,
The forest is different,
Not the old forest I used to know
With the crunchy leaves
And sunny glow.

I wonder how
The grass so green
Trees like mothers
With barely a breeze
Tucked up in the covers.

Why so dense?
The humid woodland
I look to see the sky
To see the moon and . . .
My oh my!

A shining white unicorn
Glistening in moonlight
I look again towards the sky
Hoping to see it soar,
Instead it elegantly flew by.

Skipping around the enchanting land,
Stumbling over roots and shrubs
Wondering, *what will I find*?
And seeing a dark tunnel
I thought, *I've made up my mind.*

When I get back home,
I'll say, 'Mum, I've been on a journey.'
'A journey? Where?'
'Oh Mum, I've been to a dragon's lair!'

Natasha Seaton (9)
Thomas's Battersea, London

The Crossing

The sun sinks low
Kisses the land goodnight
A beetle scuttles across the earthy ground
Follow it through the jungle I might.

The end of the forest I reach
A battlefield there before me
Metal monsters trundling along
I have no shield - I cannot see.

Monsters are charging
Advancing this way
I cross the battlefield.
Will I be okay?

A petrifying metal monster accelerates past
In the reflection of the glass - I can see
In a blink of an eye - it was gone
A frightened little girl - staring at me.

The beast has awakened
It's roaring with rage
This animal should really
Be kept in a cage.

My quest was over
It was all in the past
The door was locked
It was over at last.

Ellen Kennedy (9)
Thomas's Battersea, London

Night Journey

The spherical silver moon rose high,
Above the lethargic forest glade.
Bending bridges like liquid iron
Kissed the glinting river.

The moon - a fierce yet noble knight
Above his squire - the Earth
The city - drowsily stirring
In the chilly night.

The train clattered by.
A radiant silver light reflecting in the sky,
The moon still glowing bright,
Eerily descended into the night.

Through the windows
The moon doth glow.
'Twas like a desert - no sound at all.

Alexander Campbell (9)
Thomas's Battersea, London

The Volcano

The low grumble roared, lava spat
Poisonous gas suffocated,
Lava gushed out,
Then spurted down.
Glimmering red and orange streaks.
Devil's realm flowing with lava.
Hell had begun!

Ethan Schreyer (9)
Thomas's Battersea, London

The Boat Journey

The sun blazed down - shimmering gold,
The water splashed like elephants leaping,
The wind travelled with the boat sailing the Pacific,
Waves revealed a secret weapon,
Clouds were stunning like ballerinas,
The water camouflaged the boat,
Sand so rough, too tough to touch.
The motor of the rumbling,
The boat soars past the islands.

Quinlan Baker-Peng (9)
Thomas's Battersea, London

Graceful Steps

It took graceful steps
And silent steps
But there were no stars in the coal-black sky,
The night was dark and bare,
The only beam in the sky,
Our saviour - the great shining moon,
The sky was slate-grey,
The only sound - rats on the ground
The night was dark and bare.

Flora Stafford (9)
Thomas's Battersea, London

A Journey Around The World

From my house I rode on a bus to catch a train,
From London to Scotland where it started to rain,
Patterned kilts and matching hats they wore,
Catching a ship from Scotland to Iceland, waves roar,
Ice skating on the cold and misty ice,
The ships through the icy water's slice,
Across the Atlantic Ocean, New York is in sight,
Skyscrapers which have fantastic height,
On a coach to LA, down smooth lanes,
Driving over bridges and through dusty plains.
Get on a plane from a Los Angeles' diner,
Fly all the way to busy China,
Lots of people rushing noisily around,
I am tired and homesick so homeward-bound,
Across Asia and then to Rome.
Hip, hip, hooray I'm back at home.

Ochre Seagrim (9)
Thomas's Battersea, London

The Swallows Travel

The last birds fly away to the west
As they leave their comforting nest,
The wind blows on their feathery backs
They fly in a solid pack.
A shaft of sunlight shines on the flock of swallows
The young leave first and the adults follow.
The mother bird, her young she protects
While feasting on mounds of insects.
The two hundred miles each day
No time to delay,
Blistering winds, scorching desert they face
Winter is on the chase.
Swallows flying to their winter homes
Now they have to roam.

Kate Sullivan (9)
Thomas's Battersea, London

A Journey Of A Fire

It had been set alight,
The fire erupted, heating the coal.
The bottom of the grate started to sizzle.
Smoke started rising from the fire,
It came creeping up into the sooty chimney.
The walls of sooty bricks surrounded the
narrow passage.
The smoke never gives up
It just carries on wiggling through
the chimney.
A speck of light turns into an exit.
When the smoke says, 'Goodbye' to the chimney
for the final time.
It dissolves into cold air.

Hugo Thomas (9)
Thomas's Battersea, London

The Journey Of Death

As her ginger hair dances
And her knights with lances,
Nothing can make her happy now
Since her lover died.

As she turns weak
Her happiness leaks,
Yet her eyes,
They are still stars.

She lies in her bed,
A myriad of thoughts rushing through her head.
A white light appears,
Then the light from her face disappears.

No person will forget
The sadness and regret,
Of that accursed day
When the princess passed away.

Emily Scott (9)
Thomas's Battersea, London

The Day Going Past And The Moon Rising

The sky was gold and the sun was up.
People were rushing around.
There was noise all about in the sky and on the ground.
There were children in the park screaming and shouting.
There were ladies in the shops choosing and picking
And men at their desks, some working, some not.
The day went past, like a train going fast.
In the pink horizon the sun slid and hid behind the Earth.
Soon it became dark.
It was all silent.
The last light was extinguished
And the moon rose.

Biba Thomas (9)
Thomas's Battersea, London

The Journey Of The Moon

As dusk falls, the glistening pearl rises.
The misty ground looks like a river.
Clouds swirl casting shadows on the land,
The shadows rustle on the horizon.
Stars glistening in the jewel-blue sky.

It all goes as a cloud moves across
The round ball of silver mist.
Then there was a hoot that broke the deafening silence.
The grass swayed as a breath of wind blew.
The glistening pearl descends.

George Thomas (10)
Thomas's Battersea, London

Day Falling Into Night

As the sun disappeared over the horizon
The colours of the sky changed to a soft crimson.
Familiar daytime noises became quieter and quieter
Until there was no sound at all.
The moon rose like a brightening penny in the dark sky
And an owl broke the tranquil silence,
Day has now fallen into night.

Sophie Pennick (9)
Thomas's Battersea, London

The Journey To The Big Game

The excitement, nerves and pressure building up inside,
In the one and only beloved game, football.
It's almost time.
As thousands of fans awake
The dark tunnel welcomes the teams,
As the cold sea of blue Lions
Meet the scorching red lava of the Devils.
All this means is war!
As the heroes walk on to the green terrain,
It makes the sun vanish into its deep slumber
That awakes the moon rising from the jewelled bed.
The first sound to be heard was from a sharp and mellow whistle
Causing it all to begin, as the rock-hard metal stud rolls
The unique purple leather football coming from his golden boot.
It began. First two steps over the purple ball
And a flick to a big and guarded painted box
As a flip by a rock-hard foot
Bicycles it into the top corner of a pale-white pearl
Carved into a rectangular-shaped goal
Pinned to the ground guarding a fine wool
Which the ball gently lands into.
As the Lions start roaring the Devils stay silent
Waiting for the next move.

Jack Tollman (10)
Thomas's Battersea, London

Sleepwalker's Journey Through The Stormy Woods At Night

The wind was like an angry bull rushing at me
The lightning blinding
The thunder roaring like a lion . . .
I didn't mean to be there.

The branches leaned towards me like grabbing arms
The twigs scratching
The leaves brushing my hair . . .
I didn't mean to be there.

The ground threatening to swallow me up
Tilting wildly
Dead leaves rustling underfoot like rats . . .
I didn't mean to be there.

I needed to get out of this nightmare
Needed to get back to reality
Then suddenly . . .
I was awake finally.

Alexander Galbraith (9)
Thomas's Battersea, London

Journey Into Night

My horse gallops
along the sandy shore line
as the sun sets
behind the ocean.
My horse stops.
The water looks like it has
diamonds dancing on it.
I stare into the water
and I see my reflection
in the dancing waters.
I look up just in time to see a
dolphin jumping into the sky.
My horse starts to gallop
and she gallops to the moon.

Jacqueline Chen (9)
Thomas's Battersea, London

Winter Poem

The cold, icy wind shivers me as I turn
The corner in the crunchy snow.
Jack Frost has been everywhere.
Christmas is dawning.
I see on a cold day people wrapped in
Hats, scarves and gloves.
They huddle around fires to keep warm.
People rush through the freezing cold streets
Buying presents for their children.
Santa Claus is packing the toys
For all the good children.
The children are excited for Christmas Day
To open their surprises.
I wonder what I will get?

Alexandra Horowitz (9)
Thomas's Battersea, London

Winter

Winter is snowy,
When snowflakes drop slowly from the sky.
Winter is cold,
When you shiver in hats and scarves.
Winter is when you go shooting
And you have bonfires and roast marshmallows.
Winter is when Christmas is here
And a sparkling merry year.

Olivia Davies (7)
Thomas's Battersea, London

Hallowe'en

On All Hallow's Eve the spooks arrive
With tales of witches, ghosts and ghouls.
I stand here in fear, I hope I survive
On this moonlit night in the grounds of St Paul's.

Emerging shadows gloom in my face,
I shiver with cold, while the strong wind blows.
Frightened I run at a great pace
Over the gravestones, away from my foes.

Cosmo Taylor (7)
Thomas's Battersea, London

The Journey Of The Four Seasons

The rushing water runs through the river
As a leaf dances along to the ground,
The refreshing breeze blows silently away
And the trees' shadows glisten on the icy pond.
The autumn has come as the leaves crackle down
And all the whistling birds sing on the tops of trees.

A howling noise comes from the wind like wolves in the distance,
A snowflake falls and lands on the powdered carpet,
Winter has come for the snow is falling heavily
Like water dashing down from a tap.
Storms and ghastly winds come and go
And then it is all forgotten.

Flowers pop out all different colours
Like Jack-in-the-boxes in the fields,
Clouds disappear as the new bright sun
Appears in the distance
And all the bare trees get back their spinach-green leaves.

The summer sun has come out
Shimmering on the luscious grass,
The sea as blue as the sky
And the birds swooping around the boats,
Summer has come.
The sun is shining but soon it fades away
And we start a new adventure . . .

Alexia Auersperg (9)
Thomas's Battersea, London

Christmas

It's Christmas Eve at last!
I hope it's time to eat.
Now dinner is over,
It's time to brush our teeth,
I am so excited, my stocking's hung up,
I just can't wait to go to sleep.
It's Christmas Day hip hip hooray . . .
Let's look at what I've got today.

Imogen Carr (8)
Thomas's Battersea, London

Bonfire Night

B ang, whoosh, fizzle, pop
O range, green and blue
N ight sky bursting in flames
F ire ripping up Guy Fawkes' clothes
I watch the fireworks in wonder
R uby-red, emerald-green, gold
E choing in the night sky

N othing left of the bonfire
I n the sky the fireworks explode
G roups of children eating
H ot dogs, toffee apples and candyfloss
T onight is a night to remember.

Jamie McMullan (10)
Thomas's Battersea, London

Spring

Spring is when new babies are born
Spring is when summer is getting ready
Spring is the time to start wearing shorts and T-shirts
Spring is when the animals stop hibernating.

Spring is when the sun starts to get hot
Spring is when flowers start to spread
Spring is when the birds begin to sing
Spring is when the farmers start to scatter seeds.

Jamie Herholdt (7)
Thomas's Battersea, London

Lonely In A Corner

I'm lonely in my mind.
I forget those days when we were
Best buddies in any and every way.
But now we're confused
If we should leave or stay.
Please God, help us in any way.
Our situation is bad as we never have communication.
Now, I sit alone with no one to comfort me,
In this dusty playground.
I see my friend who is just like me.
I jump up, like 1, 2, 3, to go see her.
I'm too late for the bully has arrived with his best mate.
I stop them before it's too late.

Duvessa Bandeen (7)
Thomas's Battersea, London

Winter

Winter is a time for coats, hats and boots.
In winter you have bonfires and dark skies.
In winter people go skiing and ice skating.
Winter is when you hear ice crackling.
Winter has muddy fields.
It's the shooting season.
We have numb toes and steamy breath.
All the animals hibernate in winter.
We all love Christmas, it's a time for 'thanksgiving'.

Griffin Shelton (7)
Thomas's Battersea, London

Hallowe'en

This is a time to dress up at night
And watch the witches get into fights.
They are observed by zombies, ghosts and wolves
In the middle of full moon at Hallowe'en.
The owls screech,
The cats hiss and spit,
The comets fly through the sky,
But, thank goodness, there's some hope,
Then when I call trick or treat
To give me a wonderful pile of sweets.

Henry Tompkins (7)
Thomas's Battersea, London

Christmas

It's Christmas night,
The snow is white.
Twinkling lights shine,
Papa drinks wine.
'Time for bed,'
Mummy said.
Santa's knocking,
Where's my stocking?
I'm too excited to sleep,
Mummy says: 'Count sheep.'
How will he get through the door
To bring the toy I'm hoping for?

Coco Vulliamy Taylor (7)
Thomas's Battersea, London

Winter

Winter is my second favourite season
And this is the reason
With my mum, too scared and my dad too slow
Bad, bad, but watch me go
On a perfect set of skis
Dashing through the snow carving away from trees
I look behind me
And see my dad fall on his knees.

Joe Massey (7)
Thomas's Battersea, London

Spooky School At Night

The squirrels stare at the shining school
Paintings slowly open their eyes.
Pianos softly sing, making sounds echo through the library.
Canopic jars, lets their brains escape, when the clock strikes 12.
Fake teeth chatter on the shelf
While giant toothbrushes creak up the stairs, to scrub huge teeth.
The bells ring violently, when a bat gets hit on the head sharply.
In the gym the springboard springs over the vault
And they dance merrily on the mats.
Toy moon bears, shuffle across the floor to tell everyone the
dreadful news.

All the magic is over (it sped along so quickly).
The fun is already over.
It is 6:00.
Mr Thomas puts a foot through the door. Everything is silent!

Romey Oulton (8)
Thomas's Battersea, London

Hallowe'en

Witches, ghosts and all things spooky,
Awake this night, to give you a big, big fright.

The first witch to appear is Mary Pipstock,
Black hair, black eyes and skin as white as snow.

The second is a ghost called 'Harry the Hammer'
With a greenish, sickly glow.

The third was Frankenstein,
As tall as a door,
No seriously only 4.4.

The fourth was my mum,
To add to our meet,
We're all off,
Ready to trick or treat!

Lucas Moore (7)
Thomas's Battersea, London

The Midnight School Has Come Alive

As I creep through the school,
Library banners are flapping *violently,*
Kitchen forks are dancing *daintily* in their bowls,
Gym mats are running *excitedly* to and fro,
Classroom trays are banging *noisily,*
Paper *flying* everywhere,
Great hall piano *loudly*
Playing *funny* notes,
The outside gates swing *ferociously* hitting hedges,
Courtyard branches are *cracking,*
Dangerously falling to the ground,
The midnight school has come *alive.*

Sarah Mayne (8)
Thomas's Battersea, London

The Football Match

The whistle blew,
The wind grunted like an angry teenager,
My heart thumped
Like a Timpani drum.
The ball was swiftly passed
Through a forest of legs,
Hurtling towards me
Fast as a rocket.
My big chance to score,
Score! Score! Score!
My speedy legs spun the ball
High into the sky.
Spinning rotation, faster, faster . . .
Goalie diving frantically,
Arms outstretched like a soaring bird,
Fingertips extended.
The ball curved past him
Hitting the welcoming goal,
The goalie slammed onto the ground.
I was a hero.
Victory.
Glory.
Fame.

Arthur Vickers (8)
Thomas's Battersea, London

Evacuee

E vacuation can be very unhappy

V ery sad children

A ny person can be evacuated

C areful anyone can be sad

U nhappy parents can be sad

E vacuees can be lonely

E verybody can be evacuated.

Tharshana Selvakumar (9)
Viking First & Middle School, Northolt

Evacuee

E xcited children enjoy the countryside
V ery happy children love to work on farms
A unty Amy takes evacuees
C areless talk costs lives
U nhappy children want to go home
E verybody seems happy
E vacuees anxious about the countryside.

Raheem Rasmid
Viking First & Middle School, Northolt

Evacuee

E very child is evacuated
V ast amount of children sent away
A ngry and sad people say their goodbyes
C areless talk costs lives
U nable to talk to strangers
E xcited children are happy and proud
E veryone must watch out.

Christina Vivian (9)
Viking First & Middle School, Northolt

I Was Brave And I Was Bold

When I played football for my team,
I was the best they'd ever seen.
See me dribble, see me pass,
See me move across the grass.
I was fast and I was cunning,
I was brilliant at running.
I would score ten goals a game,
Every match would be the same.
Shots from far and shots from near,
Headers, back heels, what a star.
Fans would shout out for their hero,
When I'd made it fifteen-zero.
I was brave and I was bold
And I was only eight years old.

Amaal Mahamed (9)
Viking First & Middle School, Northolt

Only I Am Me

Only I am me
I am sweet, cute, small and adorable
I like Nintendo DS because they're cute
I like drinking Coke.

Only I am me
I like singing so much
I like to be fun, such as
I am good and smart.

Only I am me
I like Galaxy so much
That it melts
My name is Chloe.

Only I am me
I like to be kind
Sometimes mean
I love school
Sometimes every day.

Chloe Keen
Viking First & Middle School, Northolt

Only I Am Me

Only I am me,
My name is Chelsea.
I am a 9 years old,
My best friend is Daisy.

Only I am me,
I like to smile.
I like to be silly,
I get into mischief.

Only I am me,
No one is like me.
There is only one of me,
No one is quite like me.

Chelsea Rose Holman Teague (10)
Viking First & Middle School, Northolt

Only I Am Me

Only I am me,
My name is Matt,
I look like a cat,
Oh you're fat, temper, temper!

Only I am me,
I fight quite rough,
I reckon I'm tough,
Of course I'm buff.

Only I am me,
I act like Ali G.
Everyone thinks they know me,
Only I am me.

Matt Coughlan (9)
Viking First & Middle School, Northolt

Only I Am Me

Only I am me,
My game is football.
On the pitch I go,
I am a big spy,
I am nosy.

Only I am me,
My hobby is to watch films.
I love my mum,
She is a flower.
My name is Naim.

Only I am me,
I am crazy at home.
My brother is Cray.
I hate beans.
My sister is annoying,
I am nine.

Naim Suleiman (9)
Viking First & Middle School, Northolt

Only I Am Me

My name is Rebecca
I am nine years old
'You have an Afro,' I always get told
Only I am me.

I am very hyperactive
I am silly and funny
When I come out it is lovely and sunny
Only I am me.

I can be loud
I can be crazy
Sometimes I'm lazy
Only I am me.

Rebecca Sealey
Viking First & Middle School, Northolt

Only I Am Me

I am Vithiya, I am gentle,
I don't like to battle,
I smile like an angel,
I am me.

I come from Sri Lanka,
I speak Tamil,
It is so wonderful,
Only I am me.

I love to dance,
I love to drink,
I'm always funny,
I am black, I look a bit light,
Only I am me.

Vithiya Vinayagamoorthy (9)
Viking First & Middle School, Northolt